ROYAL COURT

Royal Court Theatre presents

ON RAFTERY'S HILL

by Marina Carr

On Raftery's Hill, commisioned by Druid Theatre Company, was first performed as a Druid Theatre Company/Royal Court Theatre co-production at the Town Hall Theatre, Galway on 9 May 2000. First performed at the Royal Court Jerwood Theatre Downstairs, Sloane Square, London on 29 June 2000.

Supported by The Jerwood Charitable Foundation

JERWOOD
NEW PLAYWRIGHTS

ON RAFTERY'S HILL

by **Marina Carr**

Cast in order of appearance
Sorrel Raftery **Mary Murray**
Ded Raftery **Michael Tierney**
Dinah Raftery **Cara Kelly**
Shalome Raftery **Valerie Lilley**
Red Raftery **Tom Hickey**
Isaac Dunn **Kieran Ahern**
Dara Mood **Keith McErlean**

Director **Garry Hynes**
Designer **Tony Walton**
Lighting Designer **Richard Pilbrow**
Sound Designer **Rich Walsh**
Composer **Paddy Cuneen**
Assistant Director **Andrew Flynn**
Casting **Maureen Hughes and Lisa Makin**
Production Manager **Tony Kileen**
Stage Management **Clare McCaffrey, Xenia Lewis**
Costume Design **Monica Frawley**
Dialect Coach **Andrea Ainsworth**

Royal Court Theatre wishes to thank the following for their help with this production:
Wardrobe care by Persil and Comfort courtesy of Lever Brothers Ltd.

JERWOOD
NEW PLAYWRIGHTS

Since 1993 the Jerwood Foundation's support of new playwrights has contributed
to some of the Royal Court's most successful productions, including
THE STEWARD OF CHRISTENDOM, SHOPPING AND FUCKING, EAST IS
EAST, THE BEAUTY QUEEN OF LEENANE (co-production with Druid Theatre
Company), THE WEIR, REAL CLASSY AFFAIR and THE FORCE OF CHANGE.
The Jerwood Charitable Foundation continues that support this season with ON
RAFTERY'S HILL and 4.48 PSYCHOSIS.

The Jerwood Charitable Foundation is a registered charity dedicated to imaginative
and responsible funding and sponsorship of the arts, education, design and other
areas of human endeavour and excellence. As well as the Jerwood New
Playwrights, the Charitable Foundation sponsors the Jerwood Painting Prize, the
Jerwood Applied Arts Prize and the Jerwood Choreography Awards, and has the
benefit of association with the capital projects of its parent Foundation, principally
the Jerwood Theatres at the Royal Court, the Jerwood Space in Southwark, and
the Jerwood Gallery at the National History Museum.

The Beauty Queen of Leenane
by Martin McDonagh (photo: Ivan Kyncl)

The Weir by Conor McPherson
(photo: Pau Ros)

East is East by Ayub Khan-Din
(photo: Robert Day)

The Force of Change
by Gary Mitchell (photo: Joe Dilworth)

THE COMPANY

Marina Carr (writer)
For the Royal Court: Portia Coughlan (also
Abbey, Dublin).
Other theatre includes: By the Bog of Cats
(Abbey, Dublin); The Mai (Peacock,
Dublin/Abbey, Dublin/Tricycle/McCarter,
Princeton); Low In The Dark (Project Arts
Centre, Dublin); Ullaloo (Abbey, Dublin Theatre
Festival).
Marina has recently adapted The Cherry
Orchard for The Abbey in Dublin.
Awards include: Irish Times Playwright Award
1998, The Susan Smith Blackburn Award for
Portia Coughlan, Best New Irish Play at Dublin
Theatre Festival 1994.

Kieran Ahern
For the Royal Court: The Weir (Gate,
Dublin/Toronto, Brussels, West End and
Broadway); The Steward of Christendom (co-
production with Out of Joint, including tour).
Other theatre includes: Normal (Meridian &
Project Arts Centre); The Illusion (Charabanc);
Tartuffe (Gate Theatre); The Odd Couple
(Andrew's Lane, Cork Opera House); Moll
(Cork Opera House); The Government
Inspector (Everyman Palace); The Broken Kiss
(Andrew's Lane); Lady Windermere's Fan
(Rough Magic).
Television includes: Inspector Morse, Amongst
Women, The Governor, Amazing Love Stories,
Edward No Hands, Against the Wind.
Film includes: The Last September, Titanic Town,
The Matchmaker, Pete's Meteor, Love & Rage,
Before I Sleep.

Paddy Cuneen (composer)
For the Royal Court: The Beauty Queen of
Leenane, The Leenane Trilogy (co-productions
with Druid); The Treatment, Portia Coughlan
(also Abbey, Dublin).
Other theatre includes: ; Fuenteovejuna, Peer
Gynt, Angels in America, Blue Remembered
Hills, The Sea Flight, Othello, The Birthday Party,
Chips with Everything, Battle Royal, Sweeney
Todd, A Little Night Music (RNT); Closer
(RNT/West End/Broadway); The Alchemist, The
Painter of Dishonour, The School for Scandal,
Henry IV Parts 1 & 2 (RSC); The Maids,
Company (Donmar Warehouse); The Blue Room
(Donmar/Broadway); The Iceman Cometh
(Almeida/West End/Broadway); Vassa (West
End).
Television and film includes: Golden Wedding,
Unfinished Buisness, Spirito.
Awards include: The Christopher Whelan Award
for composition in theatre.

Andrew Flynn (assistant director)
For the Royal Court: The Beauty Queen of
Leenane (co-production with Druid).
Other theatre includes: The Country Boy
(Druid); Juno and the Paycock (Gaiety Theatre).
Founded Decadent Theatre Company in 1998
and has directed with them for the past two
years.
Productions for Decadent include: One Last
White Horse, Lovers, At the Black Pig's Dyke,
Portia Coughlan, Someone Who'll Watch Over
Me, Wild Harvest.
Recently directed a production of Someone
Who'll Watch Over Me for an Irish prisons tour.

Tom Hickey
For the Royal Court: The Weir (tour/West End).
Other theatre includes: Miss Julie, Antigone,
Uncle Vanya, The Night of the Iguana (Dublin
Focus Theatre); Galileo, Of Mice and Men, The
Silver Dollar Boys, I Do Not Like Thee Doctor
Fell, Observe the Sons of Ulster Marching
Towards the Somme, The Hostage, A Doll's
House, Misogynist, The Great Hunger, The Gigli
Concert, Portia Coughlan, St.Joan, By the Bog of
Cats (Abbey, Dublin); Heartbreak House,
Waiting for Godot, Aristocrats, Three Sisters,
Double Dealer, A Midsummer Night's Dream,
London Assurance, She Stoops To Conquer,
Dorian Grey, Great Expectations, Stella by
Starlight, Lady Windermere's Fan (Gate, Dublin);
The Gay Detective, The Kiss (Project Arts
Centre); Massive Damages (Tivoli Theatre).
Film includes: The Last September, The Butcher
Boy, Double Carpet, Before I Sleep, Gold In the
Streets, Circle of Friends, Raining Stones, The
Miracle, Fools of Fortune, Big Swinger, Nuns on
the Run, High Spirits, Gothic, To the Western
World, Cal, Flight of the Doves.

Garry Hynes (director)
Founded the Druid Theatre Company in 1975.
Artistic Director 1975-1991 and again from 1995
to date. Artistic director of the Abbey Theatre,
Dublin 1991-1994.
For the Royal Court: Portia Coughlan, A Whistle
in the Dark (from the Abbey Theatre); The
Beauty Queen of Leenane and The Leenane
Trilogy (co-productions with Druid).
Other theatre includes: The Loves of Cass
MacGuire, The Playboy of the Western World,
Bailegangaire, Conversations on a Homecoming,
Wood of the Whispering, 'Tis a Pity She's a
Whore, Poor Beast in the Rain, The Country Boy
(Druid Theatre); King of the Castle, The Plough
and the Stars, The Power of Darkness, Famine
(Abbey Theatre, Dublin); The Man of Mode,
Song of the Nightingale (RSC); The Colleen
Bawn (Royal Exchange, Manchester); Juno and
the Paycock (Gaiety Theatre, Dublin); Mr Peter's

Connections (Signature Theatre, New York).
Awards include: Tony Award for the Beauty
Queen of Leenane 1998. The National Council
for Education Award in 1998 and an Honorary
Doctorate from The National University of
Ireland in 1999 for her services to Irish theatre.

Cara Kelly

For the Royal Court: The Steward of
Christendom (co-production with Out of Joint),
King Lear, All Things Nice, Young writers
Festival.
Theatre includes: Translations (Donmar
Warehouse); The Life of Galileo (Almeida);
Playboy of the Western World, Therese Raquin
(Communicado); You Never Can Tell (West
Yorkshire Playhouse); Juno and the Paycock,
Ghosts (Royal Lyceum, Edinburgh); Macbeth
(Brunton Theatre); Sharp Shorts (Traverse); The
Winter's Tale, Miss Julie (Young Vic).
Television includes: Life Support, Blood of the
Lamb, Between the Lines.
Cara has also won the Carleton Hobbs Radio 4
award.

Valerie Lilley

For the Royal Court: Blue Heart (co-production
with Out of Joint, including tour), Inventing a
New Colour (& Bristol Old Vic); Killing the Cat
(& Soho): Flying Blind (& Everyman, Liverpool).
Other theatre includes: Holy Mothers
(Ambassadors); The Mai, A Love Song for Ulster,
Factory Girls (Tricycle); Drive On (Lyric); Pig's
Ear, Skirmishes, Breezeblock Park, All My Sons
(Liverpool Playhouse); Lysistrata, Juno and the
Paycock (Contact, Manchester); My Mother Said
I Never Should, Blood Wedding, Some Kind of
Hero (Octagon, Bolton); Jane Eyre (Crucible,
Sheffield); The Cherry Orchard, The Card (New
Victoria, Stoke); Madhouse in Goa (Oldham
Coliseum); Shadow of a Gunman (Liverpool
Playhouse/Mermaid Theatre); Soapbox (Library,
Manchester); On Yer Bike (Belgrade, Coventry);
Kennedy's Children, Beggar's Opera, Camino
Real, Coming and Goings (Everyman, Liverpool);
The Plough and the Stars (Nottingham
Playhouse); Ghosts, Hamlet (Victoria, Stoke-on-
Trent).
Television includes: First Communion Day, Hope
and Glory, Peak Practice, The Rag Nymph,
Famous Five, Brookside, Missing Persons, Elidor,
Blood on the Dole, The Riff Raff Element,
Eastenders, Nice Town, Children of the North,
The Bill, Loving Hazel, Minder, The Refuge, Final
Run, Albion Market, Night of a Campaign, Give
Us a Break, The Long March, Scully, Coronation
Street.
Film includes: Priest, Scrubbers.
Radio includes: A Shout in the Distance, In the
Woods, The Secret of Fire, Son Moon and Stars.

Keith McErlean

Theatre includes: Macbeth (Upstate Theatre);
Making History (Peacock Theatre); Cyrano De
Bergerac (Gate Theatre); The Colleen Bawn
(Abbey Theatre); Cult Movie, The Return of
Travis, Louise Tripplepack, Sive (Gaiety School).
Television includes: When Brendan Met Trudy, At
Death's Door, They Shoot People Don't They,
Charming Celia.

Mary Murray

Theatre includes: Poet's Corner, In The Picture
(The Crypt Theatre, Dublin); Magic Moments
(St. Anthony's Theatre).
Television includes: The Ambassador.
Film includes: The Smiling Suicide Club,
Accelerators, Crush Proof, The Very Stuff.

Richard Pilbrow (lighting designer)

Theatre includes: Measure for Measure, A
Midsummer Night's Dream (Sir Peter Hall's Los
Angeles Shakespeare Season 1999); Ashes to
Ashes, Moonlight (Roundabout Theatre
Company NYC); The Life (Tony Award
Nomination 1997); Showboat (Gershwin
Theatre NYC, Toronto, London and USA
national tour); Tango Passion (Long Acre NYC);
The Magic Flute, The Fantastic Mr. Fox (Los
Angeles Opera); Encore (City Center); Four
Baboons Adoring the Sun (Tony Award
Nomination 1992); The Rothschilds, Rosencrantz
and Guildenstern are Dead, Zorba (Broadway);
Heliotrope Bouquet (Centre Stage, Baltimore
and La Jolla).
In 1999 and 1982 he received Lifetime
Achievement Awards for Lighting from the
United States Institute of Theatre Technology.
Founder and Chairman of Theatre Projects
Consultants of Connecticut and London.

Michael Tierney

Theatre includes: Conversations on a
Homecoming (ISDA Award for Best Actor
1993); Oranges are Not The Only Fruit (Players
Theatre, Trinity); Why The Beach Boys Are Like
Opera (Teatro Del Colosseo, Rome); Club For
Losers (Cheeky Goblin).
Film and television includes: Spáisteoireacht.

Rich Walsh (sound designer)

For the Royal Court: Four, Bluebird, The Crutch, When Brains Don't Count, Daughters, The Shining (all performed in Choice, 1998 Young Writer' Festival), Trust, Sacred Heart.

Other theatre includes: Strike Gently Away From Body, Blavatsky (Young Vic Studio); 50 Revolutions (Whitehall); The Nation's Favourite, The True Adventures of Radio One (Pleasance, Edinburgh, Jermyn Street Theatre and national tour); Small Craft Warnings (The Pleasance, London); The Taming of the Shrew, Macbeth (Japanese tour); Dirk, Double Whammy 4, Red Noses, A Flea In Her Ear (The Oxford Playhouse); The Oxford Revue (1992, 1993 & 1998, The Old Fire Station, Oxford, The Oxford Playhouse & Edinburgh); The Wizard Of Oz, The Winter's Tale (The Old Fire Station, Oxford).

Tony Walton (designer)

Theatre includes: Uncle Vanya, Taller Than a Dwarf, Guys & Dolls, Grand Hotel, Waiting For Godot, Anything Goes, Leader Of The Pack, Death and the Maiden, The Real Thing, Six Degrees of Separation, Chicago, Ashes To Ashes, Pippin, Golden Boy, Conservation Piece, The House of Blue Leaves (Broadway); Missing Footage (Old Globe); Inspecting Carol, Men's Lives (Bay Street Theatre); Lend Me a Tenor (Royal George, Chicago, Paper Mill Playhouse).

Television includes: Linda Ronstadt's Canciones de mi Padre, Death of a Salesman, Whoopi Goldberg Live, Diana Ross: For One and All (Central Park Concert); Pippin, Free To Be...You and Me, The Julie Andrews Show.

Film includes: A Doll's House, You've Got Mail, Regarding Henry, The Glass Menagerie, Heartburn, Death of a Salesman, The Goodbye People, Star 80, Deathtrap, Just Tell Me What You Want, Prince of the City, All That Jazz, The Wiz, Equus, Murder on the Orient Express, The Boyfriend, The Seagull, Petulia, Fahrenheit 451, A Funny Thing Happened on the Way to the Forum, Mary Poppins.

Awards include: Fifteen Tony nominations (including a nomination for Uncle Vanya, 2000), three Tony Awards, five Drama Desk Awards, Emmy for Death of a Salesman, five Oscar nominations for film production design of costumes, winning the award for All That Jazz.

THE ENGLISH STAGE COMPANY AT THE ROYAL COURT

The English Stage Company at the Royal Court opened in 1956 as a subsidised theatre producing new British plays, international plays and some classical revivals.

The first artistic director George Devine aimed to create a writers' theatre, 'a place where the dramatist is acknowledged as the fundamental creative force in the theatre and where the play is more important than the actors, the director, the designer'. The urgent need was to find a contemporary style in which the play, the acting, direction and design are all combined.

Devine aimed to discover 'hard-hitting, uncompromising writers whose plays are stimulating, provocative and exciting'. The Royal Court production of John Osborne's Look Back in Anger in May 1956 is now seen as the decisive starting point of modern British drama, and the policy created a new generation of British playwrights. The first wave included John Osborne, Arnold Wesker, John Arden, Ann Jellicoe, N F Simpson and Edward Bond. Early seasons included new international plays by Bertolt Brecht, Eugène Ionesco, Samuel Beckett, Jean-Paul Sartre and Marguerite Duras.

The theatre started with the 400-seat proscenium arch Theatre Downstairs, and then in 1969 opened a second theatre, the 60-seat studio Theatre Upstairs. Productions in the Theatre Upstairs have transferred to the West End, such as Conor McPherson's The Weir, Kevin Elyot's My Night With Reg and Ariel Dorfman's Death and the Maiden. The Royal Court also co-produces plays which have transferred to the West End or toured internationally, such as Sebastian Barry's The Steward of Christendom and Mark Ravenhill's Shopping and Fucking (with Out of Joint), Martin McDonagh's The Beauty Queen Of Leenane (with Druid Theatre Company), Ayub Khan-Din's East is East (with Tamasha Theatre Company, and now a feature film).

Since 1994 the Royal Court's artistic policy has again been vigorously directed to finding and producing a new generation of playwrights. The writers include Joe Penhall, Rebecca Prichard, Michael Wynne, Nick Grosso, Judy Upton, Meredith Oakes, Sarah Kane, Anthony Neilson, Judith Johnson, James Stock, Jez Butterworth, Marina Carr, Simon Block, Martin McDonagh, Mark Ravenhill, Ayub Khan-Din, Tamantha Hammerschlag, Jess Walters, Conor McPherson, Simon Stephens, Richard Bean, Roy Williams, Gary Mitchell, Mick Mahoney, Rebecca Gilman, Christopher Shinn, Kia Corthron, David Gieselmann and Marius von Mayenburg.

This expanded programme of new plays has been made possible through the support of the Jerwood Charitable Foundation, American Friends of the Royal Court Theatre and many in association with the Royal National Theatre Studio. In recent years there have been record-breaking productions at the box office, with capacity houses for Jez Butterworth's Mojo, Sebastian Barry's The Steward of Christendom, Martin McDonagh's The Beauty Queen of Leenane, Ayub Khan-Din's East is East, Eugène Ionesco's The Chairs and Conor McPherson's The Weir, which transferred to the West End and ran for nearly two years.

The newly refurbished theatre in Sloane Square opened in February 2000, with a policy still inspired by the first artistic director George Devine.

DRUID THEATRE COMPANY

Druid Theatre Company (Producer) was founded in Galway in 1975 by three graduates of the NUI Galway: Mick Lally, Marie Mullen and Garry Hynes. Since then, it has been at the forefront of Irish theatre; its foundation marked the establishment of the first professional theatre company in Ireland outside of Dublin; its regional touring pioneered the Irish touring network, and its international success has been unparalleled by any other Irish arts organisation.

Over the past twenty-five years, it has produced over 100 productions and toured extensively, both nationally and internationally. It has been acclaimed for its work on the Irish dramatic repertoire including new productions of classics by Synge, Boucicault and M.J. Molloy as well as nurturing the work of a new generation of Irish writers.

In 1979 it moved into a warehouse and converted the space into a 110-seat auditorium in the heart of Galway, which continues to be the company's home to this day. Productions which opened there and have won international acclaim include The Playboy of the Western World (1982) which The Irish Times called the definitive production, At the Black Pig's Dyke (1992), Conversations on a Homecoming (1985) and Bailegangaire (1985) which featured Siobhan McKenna in one of her finest dramatic performances. The latter two productions formed part of a major association between Druid and Tom Murphy who was Writer-in Association with the company and had four of his major works premiered in Galway.

In 1996, Druid premiered the debut work of Martin McDonagh in a co-production with the Royal Court: The Beauty Queen of Leenane opened in Galway in 1996 and has since played in London, Sydney, Dublin and on Broadway where the production won four Tony Awards, including Best Direction for Garry Hynes, the first woman to win such an award.

The company during its history has had two Artistic Directors: Hynes from 1975 to 1991 and 1995 to date and Maelíosa Stafford from 1991 to 1994. Other recent successes include The Leenane Trilogy (with the Royal Court) in which The Beauty Queen of Leenane was joined by the premieres of two other McDonagh plays, A Skull in Connemara and The Lonesome West. Druid was named Best Theatre Company at the inaugural Irish Theatre Awards in 1997. Current plans include the Druid

Debuts, a series of new plays by debut Irish playwrights. Druid Theatre Company is funded by grant-aid by The Arts Council of Ireland/An Comhairle Ealaíon.

For Druid Theatre Company

Artistic Director	Garry Hynes
Managing Director	Ciarán Walsh
Administrator	Ciara Ní Shuilleábhain
Admin Assistant	Clíona Ní Mhocháin
Production Manager	Tony Kileen

For information on Druid's activities and to be added to our mailing list, please contact us at:

Druid Theatre Company
Chapel Lane
Galway
Ireland

Telephone: + 353 91 568 660
Fax: + 353 91 563 109
email: info@druidtheatre.com

Druid is grant-aided by The Arts Council of Ireland/An Chomhairle Ealaion.

The Arts Council

Druid Theatre Company gratefully acknowledges the assistance of Galway Corporation and Galway County Council.

REBUILDING THE ROYAL COURT

In 1995, the Royal Court was awarded a National Lottery grant through the Arts Council of England, to pay for three quarters of a £26m project to rebuild completely our 100-year old home. The rules of the award required the Royal Court to raise £7.6m in partnership funding. The building has been completed thanks to the generous support of those listed below. We are particularly grateful for the contributions of over 5,700 audience members.

If you would like to support the ongoing work of the Royal Court, please contact the Development Department on 020 7565 5000.

ROYAL COURT
DEVELOPMENT BOARD
Elisabeth Murdoch (Chair)
Jonathan Cameron (Vice Chair)
Timothy Burrill
Anthony Burton
Jonathan Caplan QC
Monica Gerard-Sharp
Joyce Hytner
Dany Khosrovani
Feona McEwan
Michael Potter
Sue Stapely
Charlotte Watcyn Lewis

PRINCIPAL DONOR
Jerwood Foundation

WRITERS CIRCLE
BSkyB Ltd
The Cadogan Estate
Carillon/Schal
News International plc
Pathé
The Eva and Hans K Rausing Trust
The Rayne Foundation
Garfield Weston Foundation

DIRECTORS CIRCLE
The Esmée Fairbairn Charitable Trust
The Granada Group plc

ACTORS CIRCLE
Ronald Cohen & Sharon Harel-Cohen
Quercus Charitable Trust
The Basil Samuel Charitable Trust
The Trusthouse Charitable Foundation
The Woodward Charitable Trust

SPECIFIC DONATIONS
The Foundation for Sport and the Arts for Stage System
John Lewis Partnership plc for Balcony
City Parochial Foundation for Infra Red Induction Loops and Toilets for Disabled Patrons
RSA Art for Architecture Award Scheme for Antoni Malinowski Wall Painting

STAGE HANDS CIRCLE
Anonymous
Miss P Abel Smith
The Arthur Andersen Foundation
Associated Newspapers Ltd
The Honorable M L Astor Charitable Trust
Rosalind Bax
Character Masonry Services Ltd
Elizabeth Corob
Toby Costin
Double O Charity
The D'Oyly Carte Charitable Trust
Thomas & Simone Fenton
Lindy Fletcher
Michael Frayn
Mr R Hopkins
Roger Jospe
William Keeling
Lex Service plc
Miss A Lind-Smith
The Mactaggart Third Fund
Fiona McCall
Mrs Nicola McFarland
Mr J Mills
The Monument Trust
Jimmy Mulville & Denise O'Donoghue
David Murby
Michael Orr
William Poeton CBE & Barbara Poeton
Angela Pullen
Mr & Mrs JA Pye's Charitable Settlement
Ruth & Richard Rogers
Ann Scurfield
Ricky Shuttleworth
Brian Smith
The Spotlight
Mr N Trimble
Lionel Wigram Memorial Trust
Madeline Wilks
Richard Wilson
Mrs Katherine Yates

DESIGN TEAM
Haworth Tompkins Architects
Tony Hudson
Theatre Projects Consultants
Schal Construction Management
Price & Myers
Max Fordham & Partners
Paul Gillieron Acoustic Design
Mark Henderson
The Peter Burholt Partnership
Centre for Accessible Environments
Citex Bucknall Austin
Arnold Project Services
Drivers Jonas
Michael Gallie & Partners
Montressor Partnership

PROGRAMME SUPPORTERS

The Royal Court (English Stage Company Ltd) receives its principal funding from the London Arts Board. It is also supported financially by a wide range of private companies and public bodies and earns the remainder of its income from the box office and its own trading activities. The Royal Borough of Kensington & Chelsea gives an annual grant to the Royal Court Young Writers' Programme and the London Boroughs Grants Committee provides project funding for a number of play development initiatives.

Royal Court Registered Charity number 231242.

This year the Jerwood Charitable Foundation continues to support new plays by new playwrights with the fifth series of Jerwood New Playwrights. Since 1993 the A.S.K. Theater Projects of Los Angeles has funded a Playwrights' Programme at the theatre. Bloomberg Mondays, a continuation of the Royal Court's reduced price ticket scheme, is supported by Bloomberg News. BSkyB has also generously committed to a two-year sponsorship of the Royal Court Young Writers' Festival.

AWARDS FOR
THE ROYAL COURT

Ariel Dorfman's Death and the Maiden and John Guare's Six Degrees of Separation won the Olivier Award for Best Play in 1992 and 1993 respectively. Terry Johnson's Hysteria won the 1994 Olivier Award for Best Comedy, and also the Writers' Guild Award for Best West End Play. Kevin Elyot's My Night with Reg won the 1994 Writers' Guild Award for Best Fringe Play, the Evening Standard Award for Best Comedy, and the 1994 Olivier Award for Best Comedy. Joe Penhall was joint winner of the 1994 John Whiting Award for Some Voices. Sebastian Barry won the 1995 Writers' Guild Award for Best Fringe Play, the 1995 Critics' Circle Award and the 1997 Christopher Ewart-Biggs Literary Prize for The Steward of Christendom, and the 1995 Lloyds Private Banking Playwright of the Year Award. Jez Butterworth won the 1995 George Devine Award for Most Promising Playwright, the 1995 Writers' Guild New Writer of the Year Award, the Evening Standard Award for Most Promising Playwright and the 1995 Olivier Award for Best Comedy for Mojo. Phyllis Nagy won the 1995 Writers' Guild Award for Best Regional Play for Disappeared.

The Royal Court was the overall winner of the 1995 Prudential Award for the Arts for creativity, excellence, innovation and accessibility. The Royal Court Theatre Upstairs won the 1995 Peter Brook Empty Space Award for innovation and excellence in theatre.

Michael Wynne won the 1996 Meyer-Whitworth Award for The Knocky. Martin McDonagh won the 1996 George Devine Award, the 1996 Writers' Guild Best Fringe Play Award, the 1996 Critics' Circle Award and the 1996 Evening Standard Award for Most Promising Playwright for The Beauty Queen of Leenane. Marina Carr won the 19th Susan Smith Blackburn Prize (1996/7) for Portia Coughlan. Conor McPherson won the 1997 George Devine Award, the 1997 Critics' Circle Award and the 1997 Evening Standard Award for Most Promising Playwright for The Weir. Ayub Khan-Din won the 1997 Writers' Guild Award for Best West End Play, the 1997 Writers' Guild New Writer of the Year Award and the 1996 John Whiting Award for East is East. Anthony Neilson won the 1997 Writers' Guild Award for Best Fringe Play for The Censor.

At the 1998 Tony Awards, Martin McDonagh's The Beauty Queen of Leenane (co-production with Druid Theatre Company) won four awards including Garry Hynes for Best Director and was nominated for a further two. Eugene Ionesco's The Chairs (co-production with Theatre de Complicite) was nominated for six Tony awards. David Hare won the 1998 Time Out Live Award for Outstanding Achievement for Via Dolorosa. Sarah Kane won the 1998 Arts Foundation Fellowship in Playwriting. Rebecca Prichard won the 1998 Critics' Circle Award for Most Promising Playwright for Yard Gal.

Conor McPherson won the 1999 Olivier Award for Best New Play for The Weir. The Royal Court won the 1999 ITI Award for Excellence in International Theatre. Sarah Kane's Cleansed was judged Best Foreign Language Play in 1999 by Theater Heute in Germany. Gary Mitchell won the 1999 Pearson Best Play Award for Trust. Rebecca Gilman was joint winner of the 1999 George Devine Award and won the 1999 Evening Standard Award for Most Promising Playwright for The Glory of Living. Roy Williams was joint winner of the George Devine Award for most promising playwright for Lift Off. Gary Mitchell was joint winner of the George Devine Award 2000 for most promising playwright for The Force of Change.

In 1999, the Royal Court won the European theatre prize New Theatrical Realities, presented at Taormina Arte in Sicily, for its efforts in recent years in discovering and producing the work of young British dramatists.

ROYAL COURT BOOKSHOP

The bookshop offers a wide range of playtexts, theatre books, screenplays and art-house videos with over 1,000 titles.

Located in the downstairs BAR AND FOOD area, the bookshop is open Monday to Saturday, daytimes and evenings.

Many of the Royal Court Theatre playtexts are available for just £2 including the plays in the current season and recent works by Conor McPherson, Martin Crimp, Caryl Churchill, Sarah Kane, David Mamet, Phyllis Nagy and Rebecca Prichard. We offer a 10% reduction to students on a range of titles.

Further information : 020 7565 5024

Marina Carr
On Raftery's Hill

faber and faber

First published in 2000
by Faber and Faber Limited
3 Queen Square, London WC1N 3AU
Published in the United States by Faber and Faber Inc.
an affiliate of Farrar, Straus and Giroux Inc., New York

Typeset by Country Setting, Kingsdown, Kent CT14 8ES
Printed in England by Mackays of Chatham plc, Chatham, Kent

A CIP record for this book
is available from the British Library

ISBN 0-571-20549-6

2 4 6 8 10 9 7 5 3 1

For Dermot and William

Characters

Red Raftery
Dinah Raftery
Sorrel Raftery
Ded Raftery
Shalome Raftery
Dara Mood
Isaac Dunn

Setting: the kitchen of the Raftery household

Table
Chairs
Stairs
Landing
Door stage right leads to the yard
Door stage left leads to the pantry

Act One

Lights up on Sorrel, standing at door to the yard, listening to Ded's fiddle playing.

Sorrel That's beauhiful Ded, ya make thah up yourself?

Ded (*music stops, off*) Aye, came to me in the cornfield last nigh.

Sorrel Dinah wants to know will ya have your dinner in the cowshed or will ya come in?

Ded Where's Daddy?

Sorrel Ya know righ well he's gone huntin.

Ded Just checkin he didn't slide back in like a geenie.

Sorrel Come on in Ded, c'mon.

Ded Ya sure there's ne'er a sign of him?

Sorrel Tould ya.

Ded Alrigh I'm comin so.

Sorrel A' ya?

Ded I'm near at the duur.

Sorrel Would ya come if ya're comin, swear ya were a debutante in the high season.

Enter Ded, a man in his mid-thirties, big shouldered, long haired, bearded, filthy; cowdung all over his clothes.

Ded Quick give us the dinner and give us a buh. (*a cigarette*) G'wan, give us three.

Sorrel lights one for him. He stands there shaking, smoking nervously, shuffling in his wellingtons. He teeters, he blinks, he starts, a huge man, beaten to the scut.

Sorrel Dinah bring in hees dinner before he runs off again. There's all straw in your hair, Ded. (*Begins picking it out.*)

Ded (*flailing wildly*) Would ya lave me head alone. Can't abide anywan pawin me head.

Enter Dinah, puts the dinner on the table.

Missus, if you think I'm atin me dinner off a the table. (*voice rising in panic*) Supposin he came clackin the yard, I'd choke wud the frigh.

Dinah Humans ates their dinner off of a table, Ded. Animals ates ud off a the fluur and slapes in sheds. (*Handing the dinner to him.*) A' ya an animal a' ya?

Ded Thanks.

Shoves the dinner into his mouth, with an eye on the door and an ear cocked like a frightened bird. He manages to smoke at the same time. Dinah watches him.

Dinah God gimme patience.

Sorrel Dinah lave him, ya'll frighten him.

Dinah And whah abouh him frightenin us? You're like somewan ouha the Stone Age, Ded.

Ded Am I?

Dinah I mane when's the last time ya looked in a mirror?

Ded You're no oil paintin yourself.

8

A groan from upstairs. Ded jumps, terrified.

What's thah? Is thah him?

Sorrel Only Granny moanin in her slape.

Dinah D'ya want some a' Daddy's whiskey? Calm ya
down.

Ded D'yees have any swates? I've enough a thah.
(*dinner*)

*He holds out plate for one of them to take, edges
towards the door.*

I'll have me bag a swates now . . . when yees have a
minuhe.

Sorrel (*gives him sweets and cigarettes*) Dara brung ya
them yesterday and there's ten Woodbine and matches.

Ded But Daddy says no smokin in the shed.

Sorrel Daddy doesn't have to know everythin.

Ded Rules is rules. (*Leaves cigarettes.*) I'll go back to the
shed now.

Dinah (*coming towards him with a dishcloth*) Here, wipe
your face and hands.

He does.

(*watching him*) I allas knew wan of us wouldn't make
ud, Ded, allas knew thah. Lots thought ud'd be me.
Who'd a' ever thought ud'd be you, Daddy's golden biy
and Mother's darlin . . . what d'ya want for your dinner
tomorra?

Ded Jelly and custard.

Dinah Christ. (*And exit Dinah to the pantry.*)

Ded What's wrong a' her apart from everythin?

Sorrel She's only barkin, don't mind her.

Ded Ya want a calf nuh?

Sorrel Alrigh. (*Takes a few.*)

Ded Lovely aren't they?

Sorrel When're ya goin to come back and live in the house?

Ded When Daddy dies. I behher get back to the cattle.

> *And exit Ded as Shalome enters across the landing and down the stairs. She wears a nightdress, a straw hat and struggles with a suitcase and an armful of flowers. She is well spoken and a bit gone in her mind but with flashes of accidental lucidity.*

Shalome Goodbye Raftery's Hill. I shall not miss you. (*Strews flowers grandly over landing, stairs, kitchen below.*) Goodbye disgusting old kitchen and filthy old stairs. I shall never climb you again. Never. Goodbye Slieve Blooms, goodbye Mohia Lane, Black Lion, Ruedeskank, Croggan, Mucklagh. How could anyone be happy in a place called Mucklagh? Sorrel my darling, goodbye.

Sorrel On your travels, Granny?

Shalome I'm going back to Kinneygar and to Daddy. Goodbye.

Sorrel Bye Granny, safe journey.

Shalome (*struggles with suitcase*) Sorrel, could you help me please?

Sorrel I'll walk ya to the end a' the lane and then I'm bringin ya back to bed alrigh?

Shalome Wasn't it an awful pity your mother had to die?

Sorrel Never knew her Granny and so never missed her.

Shalome She was a lady. When she first came to the Hill we had musical evenings, card parties, dancing, always dancing, sandwiches and port wine and fruitcake all laid out in the parlour. But your father put a stop to all of that. I don't know why it is, Sorrel, but he never liked to see people enjoy themselves, a big smuth on him when everyone else was happy. Daddy was the same. (*going out the door*) I'll be away now. Wish me luck.

Dinah (*entering*) Get back up them stairs, you.

Shalome I'm never sleeping in this house again.

Dinah That's three times I'm after puttin ya down tonigh.

Shalome And I want you all to know I never loved Old Raftery. It was all just one terrible mistake.

Dinah A' ya hungry Granny? Ya allas go wanderin when you're hungry.

Shalome And do you know what Daddy said when he heard I'd married Brian Raftery?

Dinah 'I'd liefer see your white body floatin down the Shannon than for you to marry Brian Raftery.'

Shalome Oh he was master of the vicious barb, Daddy. Even his compliments had a sting. And he never came to see me after, or spoke to me, returned all my letters, don't you think that was a little? . . . a little?

Sorrel I do Granny, I do.

Shalome No matter, I'll seek him out tonight in Kinneygar and make him account for his actions. Goodbye all. (*Strews the last of the flowers grandly. Nearly out the door*) I shall send you a postcard from

Kinneygar and a long letter full of news and a bar of soap for Ded so one of these days he can wash himself.

Dinah (*bars her way*) Bed! Where's the time for me, hah?

Shalome You manage time a plenty for your sly pursuits. Now, young lady, out of my way before I give you an ass's bite. I'm going home to Kinneygar, Lord shall I ever get there?

Dinah Kinneygar, Kinneygar. Thah thick fah kip of a town. Even the dogs apologise for comin from there. Come on Granny till I warm the blue ouh a' them feeh or I'll have to take a chainsaw to them. (*Puts her sitting, kneads her legs.*) Sorrel geh her a jammy scone. Jam soothers her.

   Sorrel does.

Shalome I was going to Kinneygar, Dinah, and I forgot something.

Dinah Did ya now, ya daft auld yoke ya.

Shalome When I lived in India and Mother was still alive . . .

Dinah (*softly*) India, India. Kinneygar, Kinneygar. You're like an auld record that's stuck in the groove.

Shalome Oh but the flowers, the colours and the cool air that came down from the mountain at night. Once a man with a gorilla came to our house and the gorilla licked me all over as if I were its baby and the old man told me about the language of gorillas, how they encompassed the poetry of the sea . . . I didn't know what he meant . . . still don't. Girls! Sorrel! Dinah! Do you know what he meant?

Dinah We don't now, Granny.

Shalome And Mother came and saw me in the arms of the gorilla and was terrified it would harm me and shouts at the man and the gorilla runs down the verandah with me gripped tightly in its armpit. Next thing myself and the gorilla are looking down at Mother and the old man, we're up an orange tree. We pick orange blossom, and throw them down on Mother and the old man. Nothing will make us come out of that orange tree . . . it was a wonderful wonderful time. I couldn't have been more than three, for Mother died at the end of that summer and we left India and came back to Kinneygar.

Dinah (*to Sorrel*) How d'ya think Ded is?

Sorrel Same as ever.

Dinah A' ya blind young wan. He should be puh away. Why should I be the wan has to watch him splinter into a thousand pieces? You'll go off and marry Dara Mood and I'll be left wud thah wan racin round like a March hare in her nightdress and Ded atin hees dinner like a dog at the duur and Daddy blusterin and butcherin all the small helpless creatures a the fields. Even work horses nades a day off every wance in a moon.

Shalome (*getting up, fixes her hat, gathers suitcase*) I'll call to see you once I'm settled in Kinneygar.

Dinah Ah would ya geh up to bed.

Sorrel Leh her off, she never gets further thah the end a the lane.

Dinah Daddy'll go mad. Come on you till I settle ya again. You're tired now, aren't ya?

Shalome But I wrote Daddy I'd be arriving this evening.

Dinah Just lie down for five minutes and then ya can commence your travels.

Shalome (*allowing Dinah to lead her up the stairs*) All my life I've waited for my life to start, somehow it never has.

Dinah I know, I know Granny.

Shalome Did I ever tell you that once a German officer asked for my hand in marriage? In the Gresham Hotel. I was only fourteen, was in my school uniform.

Dinah Imagine thah, now hould the banister.

Shalome I could be in Bavaria right now. I could've met Dracula. Instead here I am. This is the thanks I get for being a good girl, these old stairs, this old hill.

> *And they're gone by now.*
> *Enter Red Raftery with two shot hares around his neck. Gun. An imposing man in his sixties. He is followed by Isaac Dunn, sly, quirky, also in his sixties, also carrying a gun.*

Red I smell cowdung . . . Ded was here wasn't he?

Isaac That's noh a cowdung smell, that's the stink a' all a' them dead sheep and cattle ya just lave maggotin the fields.

Red He was here wasn't he now?

Sorrel Aye, for hees dinner, we had to coax him in.

Red Knew I was righ. Sih in there Isaac and rest them bones. Sorrel, whiskey. (*Flings the hares at her.*) And ya may gut them, young wan.

Sorrel I will noh. Nowan ever tell ya ud's bad luck to shooh a hare, not to mind two?

Red Auld wives' tales. Skin them now young wan and gut them. I want hare's soup for me breakfast.

Isaac And he went into the lair after them and strangled the leverets. Seven little babbys all huddled in a ball. Ya don't hunt fair, Red.

Red They've the land ruined.

Isaac Ud's not the hares has the land ruined and you wud a stinkin carcass in every field. You'll turn this beauhiful farm into an abattoir.

Red (*pours two large whiskies, slams one beside Isaac*) Would ya drink thah and stop bendin me ear. Dinah? Where's Dinah?

Sorrel Settlin Granny.

Red Serve up the dinner Sorrel, there's a girl.

Sorrel goes to pantry to get the dinner.

Isaac (*after her*) Aren't ya all grown up Sorrel and I member I used thrun ya over me back.

Red None bar Dara Mood may lay a hand on her now.

Sorrel (*coming on with one plate*) There's only wan plahe in the cooker, may divide ud ouh between yees.

Red I tould Dinah Isaac'd be atin here tonigh. (*Shouts up.*) Dinah!

Dinah (*coming down*) Would ya kape ud down, Daddy. I've just goh her to slape.

Red Where's Isaac's dinner, you?

Dinah Ud's there in front a' him.

Red Whah? . . . Then where's mine?

Dinah I fed ud to the pigs. I forgoh Isaac was comin, alrigh, went clane ouh a me mind.

Red (*knocks on her head*) What's in there? Wool? Friggin moths.

Dinah I forgoh, okay!

Red What's wrong a' yees women?

Isaac Lave ud Red, sure I'm noh even hungry.

Red You want to disgrace me! Thah's what you want! Ya want word goin round thah Raftery kapes a sparse house, ya want me to have no company bar you.

Dinah Ah, would ya shuhup you're givin me a migraine.

Red Donten you talk to me like thah ya lazy rip ya, wud your skinny arms and your lunatic drames a somewan takin ya off a this Hill. I wouldn't use ya for silage.

Dinah I'm noh listenin to your pisined pulp. (*And exit Dinah up the stairs.*)

Red Come back here, you!

Isaac Christ almighy can't ya lave the girl alone?

Red Girl! She's nearly forty. (*Pushes plate to Isaac.*) You ate thah, I've no stomach after thah wan. (*to Sorrel*) Whah're you lookin ah, young wan?

Sorrel Nothin.

Red Ya want a whiskey?

Sorrel Alrigh.

Red Then get yourself a glass and stop gawkin ah me.

Sorrel goes to get a glass, sound of Ded's fiddle.

Isaac And there's Ded on hees fiddle. The lad can play, Red.

Red (*listens a minute*) So could hees mother . . . Me only son Isaac, me only son is a half wih who lives in a cowshed.

Isaac Ud's noh righ spakin abouh your own like thah.

Red Any other father'd have him in an asylum. Not me though, whah am I to do wud the farm, Isaac? Three hundred acre a the finest land this side a the Shannon and west a the Pale. And me only son and heir can't tell nigh from day, oak from ash, he'd milk a bull and drink ud in his tay and never know the differ. And I swear I seen him talkin to the corn, kissin ud and carressin ud as if ud were a golden wench swayin in the sun.

A knock on the door.

Come in.

Enter Dara Mood, a young man in his twenties.

Well if ud isn't the young fancier come to plunder the heart a me daugher.

Dara Boss. Isaac. Sorrel. (*Nods at each of them.*) Be a dirty winter for the trees is stripped already and October still in nappies.

Red (*to Sorrel*) Geh him a whiskey.

Dara Ya should clear them fields, boss, the wind takes the stink all over the Valley.

Red You look after your little farm and I'll look after mine.

Dara Ud's shockin that's whah ud is. I hear Rosie's noh well, Isaac.

Isaac I'll tell ya now Dara, women is a breeze compared to cats.

Dara Thah so?

Isaac I can do nothin righ for Rosie. She's like a prima donna ouha the operehha, wailin and flailin on the bed. Nothin would do her last nigh only hop me ouh on the fluur and her wud the whole bed to herself. And would thah sahisfy her? Noh a bih of her. There's me freezin on the fluur so I puh on me cap to trap the bih a hate goin at the top a me head and next thing Rosie's glarin ah me from under the sheets wud her paw rachin for me cap. So I says, Rosie ya cranky yoke ya, you're noh getting me cap as well, and she goes into a tantrum, tears rollin off a her whiskers and poundin the pilla. In the end I found an auld scarf used belong to the missus and tied ud round her head and thah contented her for she went off to slape after a while.

Sorrel Whah age is Rosie now?

Isaac Sixteen and a half. Her kidneys is gone.

Red Too auld for a cah. I'll puh her down if ya want.

Isaac Ya'll do no such thing. Me and Rosie is goin to the grave together like the Egyptians, have ud in me will, Philomena knows what to do, wrohe her a lehher wud burial instructions.

Red Ah would ya shuh up abouh thah stupid auld cah.

Isaac She's Padgkins Disase, same as the Elephant Man had, her bones just kapes growin, eventually all her bones'll be on the outside, kinda like a birdcage.

Red Any news from the Valley, young Mood?

Dara Only bad news.

Red The Brophy young wan?

Dara Yees heard abouh her trouble?

Red We heard alrigh.

Dara And yees heard she had the stillborn son there last wake?

Isaac The poor misfortunahe girl.

Dara Well she goes down to Clonloon cemetery last nigh and digs up the child.

Isaac Ah no. Ah no.

Sorrel I was in school wud Sarah.

Dara So the word goes ouh she's missin. Found be her father in the small hours, sittin on the coffin tryin to fade the child, couldn't say which a them bluer. Brophy throws hees coah over her and tries to take her home buh she refuses to go wudouh the child. Eventually they geh her into bed wud the corpse a the infant and she goes into some sourt a fih and dies this afternoon.

Isaac Whoever goh her into difficulty and just left her like thah should be . . .

Dara Well, here's the worst part, Brophy goes round the neighbourhood howlin for a priest. Meself and Gerrity had to hould him down, and he's whisperin thah ud was all a mistake, thah he only ever went near her the wance, thah he wanted to die as well. He's beyond in Ballinasloe now in a straih jackeh and they may watch him or he'll do away wud heeself.

Isaac You're noh sayin the child was Brophy's a' ya?

Dara I am and may God forgive him for none in the Valley will.

Red Don't belave ud. Don't believe wan word of ud. Sarah Brophy goh whah was comin to her. Now I'm sorry the child had to die, wouldn't wish thah on anywan. Buh blamin Brophy's all wrong. Ya don't know whah you're talkin abouh, young Mood. Ud's gossips like you destriys a man's good name and reputation.

Dara I heard the admission from hees own lips, wouldn't call thah gossip.

Red Ud's only your word again our beliefs, thah righ Sorrel?

Isaac Find ud hard to believe Dara and thah's noh callin ya a liar, sure Brophy has allas been the kindest a men.

Dara Ud all adds up in my mind anyway.

Sorrel Allas thought the child was Gerrity's.

Dara So did lots and called him a spineless weasel for lavin Sarah the way she was. But Gerrity tould me early on thah Sarah broke ud off wud him up on a year ago.

Red Trouble in the Valley anyway. There was allas skullduggery in the Valley. Yees should take a draught a the air up here on the Hill.

Dara Aye and keel over wud the stink a rotten sheep and cows.

Red Ah g'wan cuurtin would yees, can't kape yeer eyes off a wan another. Jay Isaac, if eyes was hands the pair a' them be stripped and pantin on the table.

Sorrel Would ya give over, Daddy.

Red Sorrel's getting embarrassed now. G'wan will yees or are ya a man ah all? Is he Isaac?

Isaac Lave the chap alone.

Red Well, what's kapin him then?

Dara I take exception to other men's talk and presumptions on a subject is none a their concern.

Isaac There's your answer, Red, was never a Mood as couldn't express heeself.

Red Sorrel is my daugher first and everythin concernin her, concerns me, includin marriage proposals. Thah said I was only jossin ya. You're too quick to hotten, and if I do laugh ah the fumblins a young lovers ud's only because I member me own. D'ya know whah ud manes to be young Dara Mood? Do ya? Manes your slate is clane, manes the muck on your boots stays on your boots and don't sape up to your unploughed soul. Manes ya know fuck all abouh the dirty world, how and why men and women fall. G'wan young Mood and enjiy yourself while your guardian angel's still around, for wan a these mornins ya'll wake and she'll be gone.

And exit Dara and Sorrel.

Isaac (*getting up*) I'll be away too.

Red Ya'll stay. Thah's whah Dinah'd like, to banish everywan and have us all gloatin round her.

Isaac You're too rough on her, way too rough altogether.

Red I have to be, otherwise she'd puh an apron on me. I'm tellin ya Isaac, give em an inch next thing you're wearin a bra.

Isaac There's worse things than wearin bras. (*Finishes drink.*) Nigh.

Red Have wan for the road?

Isaac Have to geh back to Rosie.

Red Ya prefer animals to humans.

Isaac Whah's wrong a' ya? Donten ya like your own company?

Red G'wan home to your cah, call up for ya tomorra.

Isaac Why? Ya don't even like me.

Red Whah's like got to do wud anythin?

Isaac Nigh.

And exit Isaac. Red sits there a minute, drinks, goes to stairs, calls up.

Red Dinah.

Silence.

Dinah.

Dinah Shuhup will ya, ya'll wake herself.

Red (*sings up to her*)
Come down the mountain Kahie Daly,
Come down the mountain Kahie do,
Oh can't ya hare me callin Kahie Daly,
I want to drink your Irish mountain deweeweew.

Dinah I'm radin.

Red I'm thinkin a signin the farm over to ya.

Dinah I'll geh ud in the end anyway.

Red Will I bring ya up a whiskey?

Dinah No.

Red (*mutters to himself*) Cranky cunt.

Ded's fiddle starts up, Red listens a minute, goes to the door.

Ded.

Fiddle stops.

Geh in here, you.

Ded I'm aslape.

Red Then slapewalk yourself in here or do I have to go ouh and drag ya in?

Ded appears at the door with a blanket around him, blinking, shaking, looking down.

Hould up your head you.

Ded (*does*) Is ud me fiddle playin thah's anniyin ya? I'll stop. Here, cuh off me hand.

Red Whah do I want wud your girly fiddler's hands. Stop blinkin will ya. You're noh a hare a' ya.

Ded No.

Red No. You're mad as Alfie Horgan thah's what ya are. And whah happened to him?

Ded Can I go back to the shed now?

Red I says whah happened to him?

Ded To who?

Red To Alfie Horgan, whah happened him?

Ded He choked on hees tongue in the lunatic asylum.

Red Thah's righ, he choked on hees tongue from tellin too many lies. Would you like to end up like thah, would ya?

Ded Dunno.

Red What ya mane, ya dunno?

Ded Whah's the righ answer?

Red Ya'd drive anywan mad!

Ded I should be puh away.

Red Would ya shuhup would ya.

Ded jumps terrified.

And listen here you, I know ya come in the house when I'm noh here.

Ded I do noh. I do noh.

Red Don't lie to me, I smell cowdung everywhere.

Ded I don't come in, ud's the girls makes me ate me dinner in here, otherwise I'd starve.

Red You come in here in the middle a the nigh and ya drink my whiskey and ya smoke in the cowshed.

Ded I don't. I swear I don't.

Red Would ya listen would ya, I'm glad ya come in the house even if ud's only the middle a the nigh, I'm glad ya drink me whiskey, I'm glad ya smoke in the cowshed.

Ded Then I'm glad too.

Red Christ, you're noh listenin! I'm glad! Ya know why I'm glad? Because ud manes you're noh a total animal yeh.

Ded (*confused, getting very upset*) So am I to smoke or noh to smoke? Whah? Am I to come in the house or noh? Whah? Am I to drink your whiskey or noh? Whah're ya sayin, Daddy? Just lay down the rules, don't kape changin them. Don't. I don't know whah to do to make ya happy. And I want me mother, I miss her fierce so I do. She'd kape ya away from me, she promised me she would. I'd liefer she'd pulled me into Heaven after her. (*Begins to wail.*)

Red (*through Ded's wails*) Did you take your tablets today? Would ya whist would ya? I says whist! Whist up now, ya big babby ya!

Claps a hand on Ded's mouth. Ded freezes.

24

Thah's behher. Take her handy now. Handy handy. D'ya want a whiskey?

Ded Can I go back to the shed?

Red Ya want an auld record player in the shed?

Ded I just want to go.

Red Ya want a new fiddle? The farm? Ud's yours if ya want? Jaysus, whah do ya want!

Ded Just to go back to the shed.

Red (*hits him a slap on the head*) Go then, go to be dammed!

> *Ded runs out. Red kicks the door shut after him. Enter Shalome across the landing, just out of bed, nightdress, bed socks, cardigan, suitcase, down the stairs and heading for the door.*

Red Off to Kinneygar.

Shalome (*surprise*) How did you know?

Red A wild guess.

Shalome You were always so clever, Redmond. Always. I wanted you educated, I wanted to send you away to the Jesuits, away from this terrible Hill. But no, Old Raftery wanted you rough and ignorant like himself. (*Looks at him.*) You haven't turned out the way I planned, Redmond Raftery. Why you're older than Daddy.

Red Shut the duur, Mother, have a drink before your travels. (*Red closes the door, leads her to table, pours her a drink.*)

Shalome You could've amounted to something, Redmond, if old Raftery had let me have my way. Please don't think I'm a snob, I've nothing against the people around here, they're just not our sort Redmond, never were. Old

Raftery with his dirty hurler's hands and the stink of cowdung off him. Well he never laid a hand on me. Thirty years of marriage and not once did I touch him. How many wives can boast of that? Hah?

Red I'll wager thousands.

Shalome No Redmond, your father, your real father was an English captain.

Red Ah would ya give over them lies abouh your fancy German officers and English captains!

Shalome German, English, what does it matter my dear as long as it wasn't old Raftery.

Red Who was me father? I want to hear ya say ud.

Shalome Your father, Redmond, was a beautiful looking man with soft brown eyes and the gentlest of ways.

Red No, really, who was he?

Shalome I told you he was an English officer.

Red He wasn't.

Shalome He was! He was! Don't you dare contradict me young man! He was from Yorkshire. He was lovely. I would've married him except for mean old Daddy.

Red You're a lyin witch!

Shalome Don't you raise your voice to me! I hate it young man, I hate it. I hate this world. People are just awful! They're so ridiculous with their noses and their necks and their hands and their stupid, stupid legs! I mean, what are legs actually for?

Red G'wan back to bed will ya, ya've me scutcheoned wud your lies and tales a' woe.

Shalome I'm never sleeping in this house again. I'm going back to Kinneygar and from there I shall return to India.

Red Then g'wan back to India ya mad wide heifer ya!

Shalome You're not the son I wanted, not by a long shot, and don't ever presume you are!

And exit Shalome dragging suitcase out the door. As Dinah comes down the stairs in her nightdress:

Dinah Geh back here, you! I'm noh goin after her again! (*Drinks from Red's glass.*) Christ, does anywan slape in this house any more.

Red (*takes his drink back*) Get your own glass.

Dinah You geh ud for me.

Red Alrigh, only kape your lips off a mine.

Goes to get glass. Dinah looks after him.

Dinah (*half to herself*) Skanky auld goat.

Red Ya talkin to me?

Dinah Just nohicin how auld ya've gotten. Ya've a stoop in your shoulders and a hop in your carriage.

Red You're no Easter bunny aither.

Dinah Damn righ I'm noh. No spring for me nor summer aither. I had no summer in me life, Daddy. Just auhum, allas auhum. Christ, I'm goin to die on this Hill.

Red Have to die somewhere.

Dinah The philosopher.

Red Were you drinkin upstairs?

Dinah No, I was sayin me rosary. A cuurse I was drinkin upstairs, how else could I face the lug a you. Whah were ya torturin Ded abouh?

Red He starts ballin for your mother.

Dinah Thah wan.

Red Ya remember much abouh her, do ya?

Dinah Mostly silences and headaches. May she roast like a boar on a spih in the courtyards a Hell.

Red I'll drink to thah.

Dinah And people round here still talks like she was an angel. Some angel. To everywan else maybe. Everywan bar me.

Red And me.

Dinah Ya know whah we are, Daddy?

Red Whah?

Dinah Granny was talkin abouh gorillas earlier. Thah's whah we are, gorillas in clothes pretendin to be human, goin back to bed. (*Gets up.*)

Red Ya want to go into town someday this week?

Dinah For whah?

Red I d'n know, buy a dress, get your hair done, whahever ud is yees women likes spendin money on.

Dinah Whah do I want wud a hair do or a new dress except you to ogle ud off a' me.

Red Buuks. Ya like radin. Ya want buuks?

Dinah Can get them from the mobile library. Nigh.

Red Stay a while.

Dinah Look I'm in no mood for ya tonigh.

Red G'wan then, ya contrary rip ya.

Dinah (*pauses on the stairs*) Don't touch Sorrel.

Red I won't ever . . . I swear.

Dinah Nigh so.

> *Enter Shalome with her suitcase, muck all over her.*
> *She sits on her suitcase facing the door. Red watches*
> *this a while.*

Red To Kinneygar and back already?

Shalome (*still facing the door, defeated*) I'm waiting
until it's light, dear. These Midland nights. You'd see
better in the coffin. I fell into the pigsty.

Red (*cleaning her face and hands with a dishcloth*) Ya
must have the constitution of an ox. Any other auld
wan'd be dead be now.

Shalome Far be it for me to say anything good about
Old Raftery, but I will say this much. He kept this farm
clean, you could eat your dinner off the yard if you were
that way inclined. Now it's just a river of slurry and
rotten animals. The smell from these fields. Poor Old
Raftery, I'd watch him from here, scouring the yard and
all I could think was how much I hated the shape of his
back. I was cruel to him, Red, crueller than necessary to
keep him at bay. And the crueller I was, the bigger and
sadder his eyes. In the end he just stood in ditches and
stared, died that way, standing in a ditch, staring at God
knows what.

Red He was no Padre Pio himself.

Shalome You married a good woman too, and the way
you butchered her.

Red I married a lunatic wud an antique violin and an eternal case a' migraine. If Christ heeself slid onto the pilla she'd plead the migraine. (*leading Shalome to the stairs*)

Shalome No, I can't go up these stairs.

Red If you were a cow or a sick dog ud'd be perfectly lagle to put ya ouh a' your misery, but you're an auld woman and ya can do nothin to women these days. Now geh up them stairs.

Shalome Just let me stay down here, I'll be gone at first light.

Red Just lie down, Mother, and ya can commence your travels in the mornin.

Shalome You and I, Red, what we've done to this beautiful Hill, it was beautiful and yet we're entirely blameless. What sort of monsters must we have been in a past life to suffer like this?

Red We were big loose monsters, Mother, hurlin through the air, wud carnage in our hearts and blood under our nails, and no stupid laws houldin us down or back or in.

Shalome Speak for yourself.

Red Exactly whah I'm doin.

And they're gone. Hold a minute, enter Sorrel and Dara Mood.

Sorrel He's gone to bed, come on in.

Dara Just for wan more hould a you.

Comes in, pulls her to him, kisses her, long and sweet.

In a couple more months ya'll be all mine, won't have to be lavin ya to anywan else's duur, no more jouncin haystacks or milkin parlours or tombstones.

Red has entered on the landing, stands there watching and listening.

Sorrel I may miss thah.

Dara I'll build a haystack in the bedroom for ya, and a milkin parlour. I'll plant roses on your pilla. I'll have a cherry blossom lanin over the bed tryin to kiss ya and I'll ate ya for me breakfast, me dinner and me tay. And sometimes I'll go away from ya for an hour or two, just to savour ya privahely and let ya echo through the four chambers a me heart. (*Sniffs.*) God, the smell a these filds.

Sorrel Hardly nohice ud anymore.

Dara Your auld fella seems to have lost ud altogether. I don't know how he gets away wud ud.

Sorrel He's pushin on, he's no interest in the farm any more.

Dara Such beauhiful land. Why doesn't he sell ud? I've enough saved to buy half ud as ud is and the banks'd give me the rest. Wan day I'll own all this Sorrel, you'll see.

Sorrel Daddy won't part wud ud aisy.

Dara He can't g'wan like this forever, y'ax me he looks like a man thah's finished, the way the flesh rides down hees face.

Sorrel Ya don't like him do ya?

Dara D'ya like him yourself?

Sorrel He's me father isn't he?

Dara Buh if he wasn't?

Sorrel I never think abouh him, really. D'you like your father?

Dara My father's wan sad picnic in the rain. He never speaks to me Mother, just kind a grunts and pints and sits in the corner drinkin cans a condensed milk and sighin to heeself. Me mother now is a different kittle a fish.

Sorrel Men and their auld mammies.

Dara Aye, I'm me mother's molly cuddle and glad to be. Only for her I'd be full a stingy silences like my auld fella or perverse rages like yours.

Sorrel Daddy doesn't have perverse rages, does he?

Dara I seen him cut the udders off a cow noh two wakes ago. Down in the River Field. And then he shoh ud, and then he dragged ud to the river wud a rope, a job should take three men to do. And then he pushed ud over the bank into the river. Cows is the most beauhiful creatures, gentle and trustin and curious, and they've these greah long eyelashes. This wan walked up to him and starts nuzzlin him and he goes ah her wud a knife.

Sorrel He did noh!

Dara I seen him, Sorrel, and all the time he's cursin and scramin abouh auld Raftery and the Fairyfort, couldn't make head nor tail of ud.

Sorrel Whah're ya tellin me all this for? I don't want to hear this kind a gore.

Dara There's times I fear for ya in this house. I can't wait to geh ya under me own roof, in wan piece, perfect, the way God made ya. Don't trust him, Sorrel, and don't believe him when he gives ouh abouh me, he does, doesn't he?

Sorrel Sometimes.

Dara Look, in a couple a months ya'll be safe wud me.

Sorrel I'm safe here, Daddy's allas been good to me. Ya shouldn't be sayin things like thah. Ud's noh righ.

Dara You're way too innocent.

Sorrel Look, I'm just fed up a you and Daddy givin ouh abouh wan another. I'm the wan stuck in the middle tryin to smooth everythin over. Just don't talk abouh him any more. He's auld, he'll be dead soon and you can buy hees farm and we can live and brathe and enjiy ourselves.

Dara I won't mention him again. (*Kisses her.*) I'll be away, I've a mart in the mornin.

Sorrel See ya tomorra?

Dara Ya will aye.

Kisses her again and he's gone. Red comes down the stairs.

Sorrel Oh Daddy, ya puh the heart crossways in me . . . Were you listenin to us?

Red (*paring his nails with a pocket knife*) A man can stand on hees own stairs, in hees own house, surrounded be hees own fields thah Dara Mood'll never geh hees scrubber hands on . . . And I never went after e'er a cow wud e'er a knife.

Sorrel Well, Dara's noh a liar.

Red And I am?

Sorrel Ud's so horrible ud has to be true.

Red Dara Mood has lots a rasons to lie.

Sorrel I think I'll g'wan to bed. (*He is blocking her on the stairs.*) Can I geh by . . . please?

Red Please. (*Laughs.*) Ya'll stay where ya are young wan till I give ya lave to go.

Sorrel You're drunk, Daddy.

Red I'm sober and I'm watchin you and I heard ya wishin me dead.

Sorrel I did noh.

Red I heard you and Dara Mood schemin again me, tryin to stale me farm, next thing yees'll pisin me.

Sorrel This is crazy talk, Daddy.

Red Did you gut them hares, did ya?

Sorrel I don't know how to gut a hare.

Red Donten ya? Alrigh, I'll show ya how to gut a hare.

Grabs her suddenly and holds her in a vice grip.
Sorrel struggles pointlessly against the strength of him.

Sorrel Ow! You're hurtin me Daddy.

Red (*cutting the clothes off her with the knife*) First ya skin the hare . . .

Sorrel Daddy! Stop!

Red Ya do thah slow and aisy . . .

Sorrel Whah're ya doin! Whah're ya doin!

Red (*holding her in the vice grip, all the time cutting the clothes off her*) Ya do thah slow and aisy so ya don't nick the flesh . . .

Sorrel Would ya stop! Daddy!

Red I've allas been too soft on you and look where ud's goh me.

Sorrel (*yells*) Dinah! Dinah! Come quick! Dinah! Ded! Daddy stop! Stop will ya! Dinah! Granny!

Red (*still cutting the clothes off her*) Dinah won't come and ya think Ded's comin? (*a mad laugh*) And Granny's noh comin. And your precious Dara Mood can't help ya now.

Red continues cutting the clothes off her. Sorrel gesticulates and struggles pathetically. Her voice has betrayed her. We hear the odd animal moan or shriek. Now Red has her down to her slip. He pauses, looks in satisfaction at his work.

And you all the time prancin round like the Virgin Mary. (*He pushes her across the table, cuts the straps of her slip.*) Now, this is how ya gut a hare. (*Stabs knife in table.*)

Blackout.

Act Two

Night. Three weeks later.
  Sorrel sits at kitchen table. Ded puts his head around the door.

Ded Ne'er a sign a Daddy?

  Sorrel looks at him, looks away.

Give us a buh, g'wan give us a buh.

  Sorrel opens drawer, throws a packet of cigarettes at him.

And a flame?

  Sorrel passes him matches. He lights his cigarette, smokes nervously, jauntily, quickly.

Whah're ya thinkin abouh, Sorrel?

Sorrel Noh thinkin ah all.

Ded Y'are so, can hear your brain whisperin.

Sorrel Can ya?

Ded Dara Mood comin to see ya tonigh?

Sorrel Aye.

Ded He bringin chocolahe for me?

Sorrel Doesn't he allas.

Ded That's alrigh so.

Sorrel Dinah won't talk to me any more . . . I tried to tell her, Ded.

Ded I think I may go back to the cowshed, thanks for the buh.

Sorrel Ya heard me callin, Ded . . . why didn't ya come?

Ded Ya see now, Daddy, I'm just a little bih wary a him, but same as you were to remove him, ya wouldn't know me.

Sorrel Then why don't ya remove him?

Ded I've a crowbar filed if he comes near me. I'm no girl to be played wud.

Sorrel I don't think Daddy's choosy. He just wants to bate us all inta the dirt.

Ded Ud's Dinah decides everythin round here anyway. Dinah's Daddy's cattle daler. You and me is only the cattle, Sorrel.

Dinah (*coming down the stairs with a wedding dress*) Am I now?

Ded First thing I'll do when I get this farm is peg you off of ud.

Dinah Why'd'n you just fuck back to the cowshed where ya belong?

Ded I'll go when I'm good and ready.

Dinah Ya'll go now or I'll tell Daddy ya were in here guzzlin hees whiskey and causin trouble.

Ded You tell him anythin' about me and I'll puh a mate hook through the turkey neck a ya.

Dinah And I'll ring the lunatic asylum and they'll take ya away and squaze ya like a bull calf and cut bits ouha your head.

Ded I'm getting the guards, tell them all abouh you and Daddy.

Dinah G'wan get the guards! G'wan get them! And tell them what ya done to me while you're ah ud.

Ded I done nothin to you only clane up the mess after Daddy!

Dinah Geh ouh! Geh ouh! Lave me alone!

Ded Thunderin trollop, that's what ya are!

Dinah Geh ouh! Geh ouh!

Runs for him. He runs out.

(*to Sorrel after a minute*) Ya goin to try this yoke on? (*wedding dress*)

Sorrel Ud'll be grand.

Dinah Just let me check the hem's righ. (*Holds it up against Sorrel.*) Knew ud was too long. Why'd'n ya just try the bleddy thing on!

Sorrel throws it off.

(*going up the stairs with the dress*) Well don't blame me if you're a holy show.

Sorrel You're me mother aren't ya?

Dinah Whah?

Sorrel Ya heard me.

Dinah You'd want to stop all this nonsense and moonin abouh or your groom'll flee the altar.

Sorrel Suppose I allas knew ud . . . buried in me though.

Dinah Our mother died givin birth to you . . . now stop all a this for your own sake.

Sorrel You and Daddy.

Dinah Whah're ya on abouh?

Sorrel (*a suppressed sob*) Nothin I suppose . . .

Dinah You're nervous about the weddin, aren't ya now?

Sorrel Aye.

Dinah Don't you worry, ud'll all be fine. I'll make sure your dress is beauhiful and I've all the flowers planned. Cornflowers for your hair, them is your favourihe, aren't they now?

Sorrel Aye.

Dinah And a big bunch a lillies on the altar, and Daddy says we're to spare no expense, he wants ya to have a astoundin day . . . he can be very good, Daddy, can't he now?

Sorrel Yeah.

Dinah And we're to go into Brown's Hotel wan a these days to decide on the menu for the weddin breakfast and even Ded says he'll come to your big day. Isn't thah somethin, Sorrel?

Sorrel I won't be comin back to this Hill ever again, ya may come and visih me in the Valley.

Dinah Sure I will, sure I will Sorrel . . . anythin . . . anythin to gladden ya up.

Sorrel Why'd'n you ever get married?

Dinah No wan ever axed me, besides who'd look after yees all?

Sorrel Can look after meself.

Dinah Now ya can, buh when ya were a babby, nowan to mind ya except me. Granny was allas useless.

Sorrel Whah was me mother like?

39

Dinah Whah was she like? Good lookin, like you. I take after Daddy.

Sorrel Whah else abouh her?

Dinah She was allas sick, long as I can remember anyway . . . lyin in the back parlour wud a dish cloth on her head . . . never liked the woman, may god forgive me.

Sorrel Did ya noh.

Dinah Fierce selfish, and Ded was her favourihe. Any attention I goh was from Daddy. He used take me up the fields wud him, up on hees shoulders, thought I was a giant. I went everywhere wud him, he'd be mendin fences and I'd be playin wud me dolls beside him, or savin the hay, he'd throw me up on the haycocks and I'd roll down them and he'd ketch me, taught me to fish . . .

Sorrel Taught me to fish too.

Dinah Taught me all the name a the trees, ash behind the house, sycamore in the Church Field, yew and oak in the Calla, sycamore, elder, blackthorn, the River Field, beech the Lower Field, beech the Haggard, beech the Fairyfort . . . I remember the names a trees like nowan. . . . And I'd make him tay before I was the size a the range, he'd have to lift me up and hould the kettle so I wouldn't scald meself, and then he'd drink it, swill it round his mouth and say, well I declare that's the best cup a tay this side a the Shannon and west a the Pale. And I'd stand there watchin him, as proud a meself . . . He knew how to build up a child's heart . . . Daddy, never forgeh him for thah.

And exit Dinah up the stairs with wedding dress.
Enter Red and Isaac, guns, hunting bags and flasks.

Red Ah Sorrel, you're up and abouh, ya over thah flu?

Sorrel And whah flu is thah now?

Isaac Musta been a fierce dose ya goh.

Sorrel Oh fierce, Isaac, fierce.

Red Pour us whiskeys, there's a girl.

Sorrel goes to pantry, comes back with two glasses.

Red Seems to me be the longest winter of all the winters I have lived.

Isaac I remember worser winters than this wan.

Red This wan fluurs them all. (*to Sorrel*) Jine us, why don't ya.

Sorrel looks at him, goes up the stairs.

Isaac Eighy-wan, now thah was a winter put manners on lovers, the whole mountain and valley courtin with gloves on. Eighy-wan, the missus dead and snow to the rafters, couldn't geh up the road to bury her. Slept beside her three nights tryin to warm her up. Be asier hotten the wastes of Antarctica or melt the pakes of Everest.

Red I'd say thah.

Isaac Anyway, if'n ya ax me winters has nothin to do wud weather. I seen men freeze on Midsummer's Day. Jack Frost nor the Ice Quane does be sittin on the front duur a their heart.

Red There's gravel in thah . . . me father, now come the winter'd sih out there in hees Morris Minor, member ud?

Isaac I do.

Red Called ud hees smokin saloon, he'd sit there for hours, lookin at nothin . . . d'ya know I can't ever remember talkin to him.

Isaac I often spoke to him and I passin.

Red And whah used he talk abouh?

Isaac The weather, the football, the hurlin, who's dead, who's dyin, normal conversation.

Red Hmmh.

Isaac Sure wasn't he the greahest hurler ever to come ouha this county, and then wan Sunday he doesn't show up. Shockin bad blood over thah and the tame creahed around him.

Red Over somethin thah was said at the time, that's what thah was abouh.

Isaac Forgeh now, it's a long time ago.

Red Like hell ya forgeh and you wud the biggest lugs in the parish. Ud was all over somethin thah was said abouh me mother and abouh me.

Isaac Only auld gossip . . . ya heard Brophy drank a mug a weedkiller.

Red I heard thah.

Isaac Still find ud hard to believe.

Red Sure, even if he done to Sarah what they're all sayin he done, what did he have to go and down a mug a weedkiller for?

Isaac Mebbe the lavins of Christian dacency made him do ud.

Red Wouldn't your auld Christ forgive him?

Isaac They say he forgives everywan exceptin devils. Dependin on whether ya'd class Brophy as a devil or noh . . . still it's a loh to ax forgiveness for.

Red Aye, if you're wan a them as hankers after forgiveness.

Isaac Me own daugher now . . .

Red Philomena.

Isaac Don't see much of her any more, buh I can't imagine how any father could do thah to hees daugher.

Red Well, I can't imagine anywan wantin to do anythin to Philomena.

Isaac The bleddy nerve a ya talkin abouh Philomena like thah!

Red Ah I'm only jokin ya! Buh admih ud, the girl's a wagon, noh her fault, but she is. Where's your sense a humour, the cah taken thah too?

Isaac Talk about your own how ya like, but noh about mine.

Red Can't a man make a joke any more?

Isaac Brophy disgusts me! Monster, that's whah he is! And them's my unchristian thoughts on the mahher.

Red And doesn't your God make monsters too, for all the righteous to look down on? Didn't he create Lucifer for the sole pleasure of flingin him ouha Heaven?

Isaac Monsters makes themselves. They were hopped into the world clane as the next. The Grakes however has a different opinion of the mahher. Zeus and the missus . . . whah was her name? . . . Hera, Zeus and Hera, sure they were brother and sister and they goh married and had chaps and young wans and the chaps and young wans done the job wud the mother and father and one another, and sure the whole loh a them were ah ud mornin, noon and nigh, I suppose they had to populahe the world someway. Is ud any wonder the stahe a the country and them for ancestry. (*Finishes his drink.*) I'll be away.

Dinah (*coming down the stairs*) Home to Rosie, Isaac?

Isaac Rosie died last nigh, five past three, peacefully. I'm thinkin of havin a waistcoah made ouha her.

Dinah So ya can stroke her from time to time?

Isaac Mebbe . . . nigh.

Dinah Nigh, Isaac.

And exit Isaac.

Red Well the young wan's up . . .

Dinah just glares at him.

She alrigh is she?

Dinah She's noh wan bih alrigh . . . just cries and cries, won't ate anythin, just keeps takin a bah.

Red She's only sulkin.

Dinah Wan thing I axed you to do me whole life! Lave Sorrel alone. Whah we need here is the guards, the social workers, the whole shootin loh a them. I'm thinkin a tellin Dara Mood the class of an animal he'll have for a father-in-law.

Red You start peggin muck, I've plenty to peg back.

Dinah Noh again me ya haven't. I'll get Sorrel to back me.

Red Lave the young wan ouh of ud.

Dinah Was you brung her in! Where are ya goin to stop Daddy? Where?

Red At the end a cuurse, where else.

Dinah And where the hell's thah?

Red Would ya stop grousin over nothin. I barely went near her.

Dinah Barely did ya! There's marks on her as hasn't haled in three weeks!

Red You didn't hear the things she said abouh me.

Dinah For eigheen year I watched thah wan like a hawk, protected her from you, and what does the stupid little bitch go and do? Gives ouh abouh you under your own roof. Christ, doesn't she nohice anythin? Doesn't she know you be paddin round the duurs and landins, wud your cloven toes, spyin on everywan, waitin to pounce? I seen pictures a your toes in books, books abouh devils wud their toes all stuck together.

Red You're involved here too missus, layin ud all on me, I barely touched her.

Dinah (*dives for his neck, throttles him, he laughs*) Don't small talk me you! Save ud for them as doesn't know ya! Whah are ya! Whah are ya!

Red You're jealous is all.

Dinah Jealous a you is ud, wud the big stumpy jaw a black molars on ya!

Red You're no Marilyn Monroe aither, missus.

Dinah I'm noh even forty till next year and look ah the stahe a you, sure you're eligible for the auld age pension and ya need a hearin aid.

Red I hear fine so I do.

Dinah Why couldn't ya a just lave her alone? The wan perfect thing in this house.

Red I was only puttin manners on her, somewan had to, you've leh her run wild . . . here. (*Gives her a big wad of money.*) G'way and spend thah for yourself.

Dinah (*takes the money, puts it in her pocket*) Ya think a big fist a dirty tenners solves everythin.

Red Ya want more? How much do ya bleddy want?

Sorrel crosses the landing.

Dinah Ah Sorrel, ya comin down?

Sorrel Goin for a bah.

Dinah Ya'd wan already today and two last nigh.

Sorrel Well, I'm goin for another wan.

Red Ya may lave me some hot waher for my bah.

Dinah What do you want a bah for?

Red Never you mind now, nosey parker.

Dinah To smell nice for me is ud?

Red Can't a man dunk heeself in his own bah withouh a runnin commentary?

Dinah All the Shannon wouldn't wash you clane, Daddy.

Red (*shouts up to Sorrel*) Young wan!

Sorrel Whah?

Red High time you goh dressed and joined the land a the livin.

Sorrel I'm noh well.

Red We'll let bygones be bygones young wan. Just apologize to me now and we'll say no more abouh ud.

Sorrel Apologize to you!

Dinah Ud's high time yees were greah agin, come down and make ud up wud him, I'm the wan stuck atwane yees tryin to keep the pace.

Red Mother Teresa's only trottin after ya. Get down here young wan, I've had enough a your ghost act and your double dalin and your vicious attack on me.

Sorrel Just lave me alone. (*And exit Sorrel to bathroom.*)

Red Is she goin to start spreadin lies?

Dinah Doubh ud . . . she's a Raftery, a double Raftery, well versed in subterfuge.

Red Look, Dinah, we'll turn things round here, clane them fields, get the ground ready for spring.

Dinah We should be allas workin the farm and there'd be none a this, everythin goes bockety when we don't be ouh workin the fields and the cattle and the pigs.

Door opens. Enter Shalome, bedraggled, lugging her suitcase after her.

Shalome (*sticking her head around the door*) Oh sorry, wrong house. (*Goes back out.*)

Dinah Geh in here, you. (*Goes after her, pulls her in.*)

Shalome No, let me go, I thought I was on the road to Kinneygar.

Red Come in before ya ketch ammonia.

Shalome (*allowing herself to be brought in*) Kinneygar, will I ever get back there?

Dinah It's only twenty mile down the road. If ya really wanted to go there ya'd go, it's all a figary just to geh at me.

Shalome You're not as nice as me to Sorrel, poor little Sorrel, I wanted to stop it. Is she alive still?

Dinah Sih down will ya till I get ya a bun.

Shalome When I tell Daddy all I've had to put up with. Did you know Daddy used to take me boating on Lilliput Lake? Every summer, boating on the lake, we don't have summers like those any more, dragonflies on the water, the sun bursting the sky, and Daddy would row and say, are you tired, darling? And I'd lie there looking at him through my fingers, and once he said, Shalome look at the heron feeding in the rushes. Shalome. No one has ever pronounced my name nicer than Daddy.

Ded (*off, shouts outside the door*) You and your fuckin Daddy! D'ya ever talk abouh anythin else do ya!

Red (*goes to door, opens it*) Geh in here you. Ded! I said geh in. And where's your shirt gone to? (*Pulls him in.*) Dinah, geh him wan a my shirts.

Ded What do I want wan a your stinky shirts for?

Red Ya been skippin your tablets again.

Ded What's tablets got to do wud anythin, there's nothin wrong a me.

Red Come on sih in, have a whiskey till we warm ya up.

Ded (*to Shalome*) And you missus, where the fuck were you when ya were naded!

Shalome Such filthy language in my presence. You apologise this minute, young man.

Ded I'll tell ya where ya were, up in your bed, dramin a your Daddy. Perverts the loh a' yees.

Red That's enough poetry ouha you now.

Ded I was the wan had to do ih all. I was the wan had to take Dinah to the cowshed, member thah, do ya, Daddy?

Dinah (*on the stairs*) Aye he remembers alrigh Ded.

Ded And you (*to Shalome*) suckin your Fox's Glacier Mints and playin patience and the roars a Dinah and blood and every bleddy thing comin ouha her.

Red I says thah's enough Ded, you're ravin is all, thah's whah happens when ya don't take them tablets, drink up your whiskey there, good lad, ya want a buh do ya? (*Offers him a cigarette.*)

Ded And do yees know the worst, the worst of ih all? Mother never spoke to me again, I never seen her again. Yees wouldn't even leh me go to her funeral.

Dinah Here puh this on before ya freeze. (*shirt*)

Ded Are you still cross wud me, Dinah?

Dinah And whah would I be cross wud ya abouh?

Ded I d'know . . . everythin . . . I was only doin whah Daddy tould me, buh I never done nothin to you sure I didn't.

Dinah No ya didn't, Ded, ya never done nothin to me.

Ded Thah's alrigh so, I geh inta a swill sometimes, geh all mixed up abouh thah time buh I'm noh an animal sure I'm noh?

Dinah No, it's not you is the animal, Ded.

Ded As long as I never harmed ya.

Red Would ya shuhup would ya! No wan harmed anywan. Nowan!

Ded I'm next amn't I? It's my turn next.

Red And whah would I want wud you, wud your sissy fiddle, ya can't even look after a shed a cattle.

Ded I've axes and billhooks and a plastic yoke a strychnine I'll peg in your eye if ya come near me. I'm never comin inta this house again. Dinah, ya may lave me dinners at the shed duur. (*to Red*) And you, you're barred from the cowshed. (*And exit Ded.*)

Red Jaysus whah a threat. (*to Dinah*) Go after him you, and see he's alrigh.

Dinah goes out after Ded.

Shalome He's an absolute disgrace that fellow, you didn't give him a proper rearing, Red.

Red He was reared as well as the next. Ded's me thorn. Every man has wan, every woman too. I'm yours. G'wan to bed will ya, ouha me sigh.

Shalome I'm hungry.

Red A' ya, Dinah'll fade ya when she comes in.

A knock on the door.

Ud's on the latch.

Enter Dara Mood. Fiddle music starts up from the cowshed.

Dara Boss. (*Nods.*) Mrs Raftery. (*Nods.*)

Shalome Shalome, call me Shalome, that's my name.

Red (*shouts up*) Sorrel, himself is here.

Shalome You'll make someone very happy Dara Mood, but it won't be Sorrel because you see we're strange creatures up here on the Hill. And strange creatures, aberrations like us, don't make for lifetime companions.

Sorrel That's enough ouha you Granny.

Red I suppose you're wonderin what's goin wud her?

Dara What do ya mane?

Red Don't play innocent wud me, Mood. Ya know righ well I'm not goin to peg her into the world like a broken cup. (*Produces papers and envelope from his pocket.*) There's the deeds a Fifty Acre there and a cheque for twenty grand. (*Throws them on the table.*)

Dinah (*entering*) Me or Ded never goh any fifty acre or twenty grand.

Red (*to Sorrel*) That's all you're getting so don't come lookin for more when they put me bones down.

Dinah Come on Granny, and lave them to their bribery and blackmail.

Shalome Could I have some toast and jam first?

Dinah When you're settled ya can.

As they exit up the stairs:

Red And I'm tellin ya now, Mood, ya may keep your trap shuh as to how I run me farm, see how well you'll manage now you've a hundred acre to work.

Dara I'm not sure I want your fifty.

Red Sure ya do.

Dara As a mahher a fact I don't.

Sorrel Dara!

Red You're a bigger fool than Ded.

Sorrel Take the Fifty Acre, Dara, and the cheque. Look, you're allas sayin if ya'd more land what ya'd wud ud. now's your chance.

Dara I'll buy me own land Sorrel, don't like handouts, especially them that's given in such an ungracious way.

Red Oh the pride a the Scrubber Moods.

Sorrel Well ud's mine. I'm owed ud. I'll take ud.

Red Owed ud are ya! And whah have you ever done to deserve me two best fields?

Sorrel Done plenty so I have.

Red Aye, ya have, ya little upstart ya.

Dara If you want them Sorrel, take them, they're yours to take buh I won't touch them.

Sorrel I don't need you to tell me whah I can do. They're mine and dearly paid for. (*Takes the papers and cheque, runs upstairs with them.*)

Red That's righ, take the money and run, ya kite ya. Be careful young Mood, for I've rared up an avaricious little thing wud pound signs lewin in her eyes.

Dara You've the knack a reducin everywan to dirt.

Red No lad, you've ud all wrong, ya see women, ya may watch them, watch your back lad for fear they stick a knife in ud.

Dara You're nothin only a bull on crutches.

Red (*drinks a large whiskey*) G'wan and cuurt your greedy bride and grow rich on the fah a my fields. There was a time I'd shooh a man who'd dare to walk across me River Field withouh permission. Noh any more. Ud's yours now and ya may breed rats on ud for all I care. (*Puts on his coat, gets his gun, hunting flask.*)

Dara I'll noh touch your River Field, Red Raftery, noh if ud was harvestin nightingales and gold.

Red Big words from the small farmer. Raftery's Hill fed yees all through the Greah Hunger, sould yees yeer fifty acre a scrub and marsh, 1923. You'll take me River Field young Mood, and me churchyard field, and me daugher, for the Moods was ever opportune and you're wan a' them.

Dara You'll never see my plough on your cursed land.

Red (*as he exits*) You may see mine on yours.

Dara Whah?

Red is gone.

(*goes to stairs, calls up*) Sorrel?

Sorrel comes onto the landing.

Dara What's goin on here?

Sorrel There's natin goin on here except you decidin things in swell a pride thah concerns me.

Dara Your father, Sorrel, I have to say ud. I can't abide the man.

Sorrel Well, hees blood runs through me so what you're really sayin is ya can't abide me.

Dara Ya know righ well that's noh whah I'm sayin. (*Goes up the stairs to her.*)

Sorrel Go way from me you now.

Dara Sorrel!

Sorrel No! Go way from me! There's natin wrong a Daddy. Ud's you! Think ya know everythin abouh everywan! Well, ya know natin, Dara Mood.

Dara Then tell me.

Sorrel Why couldn't ya a just taken the land and the money? Why couldn't ya a? Ya gone and ruined everythin so ya have. Anyway I don't want to be a small farmer's wife. With this fifty acre we'll have somethin. (*Shakes papers at him.*) And wud this (*cheque*) we'll be rich and have standin in the communihy instead a been scrubbers from the Valley.

Dara So that's whah I am, a scrubber from the Valley.

Sorrel Ud came ouh wrong.

Dara Buh ud came, strange that's the exact phrase your father used noh ten minutes ago. I allas thought I came to ya as an equal, Sorrel.

Sorrel There ya go again wud your stupid pride! Only for you ud'd all a gone smooth, allas givin ouh abouh Daddy and under hees very roof and all. Ya know of old hees manner is gruff, buh he manes natin by ud. He's good at the back of ud all, leastways hees instincts are, and for you to be puttin him down to hees daugher is wrong! Same as I was to start in on your family, how'd ya like thah?

Dara Well, if your Daddy's as good as ya say he is mebbe ud's him ya should be marryin.

Sorrel Well, I know wan thing, I won't be marryin you.

Dara That's a bih extreme isn't ud?

Sorrel Ya've ruined everythin, Dara Mood, ya gone and ruined everythin.

Dara Ruined whah?

Sorrel I don't know. I don't know anythin any more . . . The world's gone ouh like a ligh and I can't see righ abouh anythin any more.

Dara Let's not figh.

Sorrel Ud's over, Dara. Don't come here again. (*And exit Sorrel from the landing.*)

Dara Whah? . . . What do ya mane? . . . Sorrel?

Dinah crosses the landing and down the stairs.

Dara What's goin on in this house?

Dinah We're just tryin to live like everywan else, don't ya know how hard thah is sometimes, Dara Mood, just to live. What's wrong a ya? A tiff wud Sorrel?

Dara Sorrel's not righ in herself this last few weeks, she's gone schaways altogether. Did somethin happen her?

Dinah (*Pouring whiskey*) Ya want wan.

Dara Naw.

Dinah Sorrel'll be fine. She's young, her whole life ahead a her wud a beauhiful young husband like you by her side. Me now, what do I have to look forward to? (*Drinks.*)

Dara Sure, hadn't you the pick a all the lads wan time? didn't ya dangle me own brother on a string for the longest while. . . . he still axes after ya.

Dinah How is he?

Dara The finest. Another babby comin in June.

Dinah That'll be three he'll have.

Dara Aye ud will.

Dinah In another life they'd have been mine . . . I brok ud off wud Jimmy fierce sudden and fierce hard . . . things was rickety for me thah time. Ud's allas the wans you're fondest of ya drop the axe on . . . Sorrel'll be fine, I'll knock sense into her, g'wan home and come back in a few weeks.

55

Dara Alrigh, if ya think I should stay away for a while.

Dinah I do.

Dara Nigh so.

Dinah Nigh, Dara. (*Looks up the stairs and exits.*)

Dinah sits at table, Shalome comes onto landing and down the stairs in Sorrel's wedding dress.

Shalome (*to herself*) You left Kinneygar in your wedding dress so it's only right you should return in it.

Dinah Christsake Granny! That's Sorrel's! You've ud ruined.

Shalome I'm going back to Daddy in Kinneygar.

Dinah Ya'd put years on Father Time heeself.

Sorrel comes down the stairs.

Sorrel Lave her, Dinah.

Dinah And leh her ruin your dress in the yard and the lanes?

Sorrel I won't be needin ud.

Dinah What do ya mane, ya won't be needin ud?

Shalome escapes out the door.

Shalome Bye Raftery's House, bye Raftery's Hill . . .

Dinah Don't come back here tonigh you! I'm not puttin ya down again. (*Slams door on her.*) Whah were ya fightin wud Dara Mood abouh?

Sorrel Just tould him I won't be marryin him is all.

Dinah And why noh?

Sorrel Why do ya think?

Dinah Ud's not the end a the world just because hands was laid on ya thah shouldn't a. Why couldn't ya a just been more careful?

Sorrel So ud's all my fault!

Dinah I'm noh sayin ud is, only I never had anywan lookin ouh for me the way I looked ouh for you.

Sorrel Some lookouh you are and ya listenin behind the duur to the whole thing.

Dinah For eigheen years I watched you and minded you and kept ya safe! Ya know how many wishes and drames thah is brushed aside. Eigheen years, the best part a me life and noh wan bih a grahitude from you! No, ya go and fling ud in me face. I had a whole life before you came along missus, nowan ever stood up for me. Ya know whah my Mother done? She sent me into the bed aside him. I was lanin on the fridge in the pantry and she comes in behind me and says ouh a nowhere, you're to sleep in wud your father tonigh. She didn't want him so she sends me in. I was twelve.

Sorrel And since?

Dinah What do ya mane, 'and since'?

Sorrel Innocent as a lamb aren't ya? Don't think I don't know your and Daddy's nocturnal carryin ons. Whah is ud? Wance a month? Wance every two months? A period a guilt and atonement for yeer sins and then yees are back ah ud again.

Dinah So we do ud from time to time, allas in the pitch dark, never a word, ud's nowan's bleddy business. Who's ud hurtin? And we want ud to stop. You don't believe thah. You don't believe anythin good abouh me and Daddy, we don't aither buh we want ud to stop. Ud's just like children playin in a field ah some awful game before laws was made, buh you're noh goin to end up like me, you're goin to marry Dara Mood and geh off a' this hill if I have to run ya off.

Sorrel Ya'd have me in a poh a lies wud Dara Mood.

Dinah Ud's not lyin, ud's just noh tellin him things. Ud's just sayin the opposite of whah you're thinkin. Most goes through their whole life sayin the opposite a whah they think. What's so different about you?

Sorrel I won't do ud.

Dinah Then what'll ya do? Rot up here? Go tearin round in your nightdress like Granny?

Sorrel I won't pretend wud Dara.

Dinah Well, ya behher noh start tellin him lies abouh us. We're a respectable family, we love wan another and whahever happened ya happened ya be accident. D'ya honestly think we'd harm wan another?

Sorrel Spare me your Legion a' Mary canter. We're a band a gorillas swingin from the trees.

Enter Red with Shalome in muddied wedding dress.

Red Would yees look ah the stahe a' Sorrel's dress.

Shalome (*to Red*) Do you think will Daddy recognize me after all these years?

Red I tould ya a hundred times he's dead. Dead, Mother! Dead.

Shalome No . . . you must be thinking of someone else.

Red Don't ya remember hees funeral? Ya took me, I must a been whah? Twelve, thirteen, the army out blowin their bugles, a woman came up to me and said, God, but you're the spih of him. (*Laughs.*)

Shalome Daddy dead? What a lark. Daddies never die, they just fake rigor mortis and all the time they're throwing tantrums in the coffin, claw marks on the lid.

Dinah Did ya ketch anythin?

Red Only this auld bird. I nearly shoh her.

Dinah Why didn't ya?

Red (*to Sorrel*) I hope you knocked some sense inta young Mood.

Sorrel Oh I sourted him ouh Daddy, don't you worry, I sourted him ouh for ever more.

> *Music from Ded's fiddle, and fade.*
> *End.*